D1568797

Football Superstar
Tom Brady

by Jon M. Fishman

BUMBA BOOKS™

LERNER PUBLICATIONS ◆ MINNEAPOLIS

Note to Educators

Throughout this book, you'll find critical-thinking questions. These can be used to engage young readers in thinking critically about the topic and in using the text and photos to do so.

Lerner Publications Company
A division of Lerner Publishing Group, Inc.
241 First Avenue North
Minneapolis, MN 55401 USA

For reading levels and more information, look up this title at www.lernerbooks.com.

Library of Congress Cataloging-in-Publication Data

Names: Fishman, Jon M., author.
Title: Football superstar Tom Brady / by Jon M. Fishman.
Description: Minneapolis, Minnesota : Lerner Publications, [2019] | Series: Bumba Books — Sports superstars | Audience: Ages: 4–7. | Audience: Grades: K to Grade 3. | Includes bibliographical references and index.
Identifiers: LCCN 2018016820 (print) | LCCN 2018028099 (ebook) | ISBN 9781541542990 (eb pdf) | ISBN 9781541538498 (Library bound : alk. paper) | ISBN 9781541545779 (Paperback : alk. paper)
Subjects: LCSH: Brady, Tom, 1977– Juvenile literature. | Football players—United States—Biography—Juvenile literature. | Quarterbacks (Football)—United States—Biography—Juvenile literature.
Classification: LCC GV939.B685 (ebook) | LCC GV939.B685 F57 2019 (print) | DDC 796.332092 [B] —dc23

LC record available at https://lccn.loc.gov/2018016820

Manufactured in the United States of America
1-45032-35859-6/20/2018

Table of Contents

Team Leader 4

Football Gear 22

Picture Glossary 23

Read More 24

Index 24

Team Leader

Tom Brady is a superstar quarterback.

He plays for the New England Patriots.

Tom played many sports as a kid.

He played football and baseball in

high school.

Why do people play sports?

Tom liked football best.

He played football at college

in Michigan.

Then he joined the New England Patriots.

He became the team's quarterback.

Tom worked hard.

He helped his team get better.

How can people make a team better?

The Patriots played in the Super Bowl eight times. They won the Super Bowl five times.

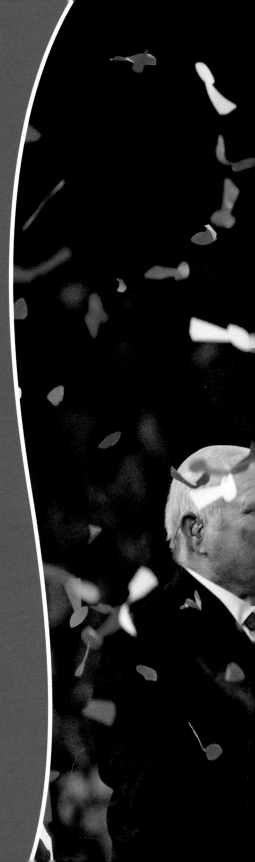

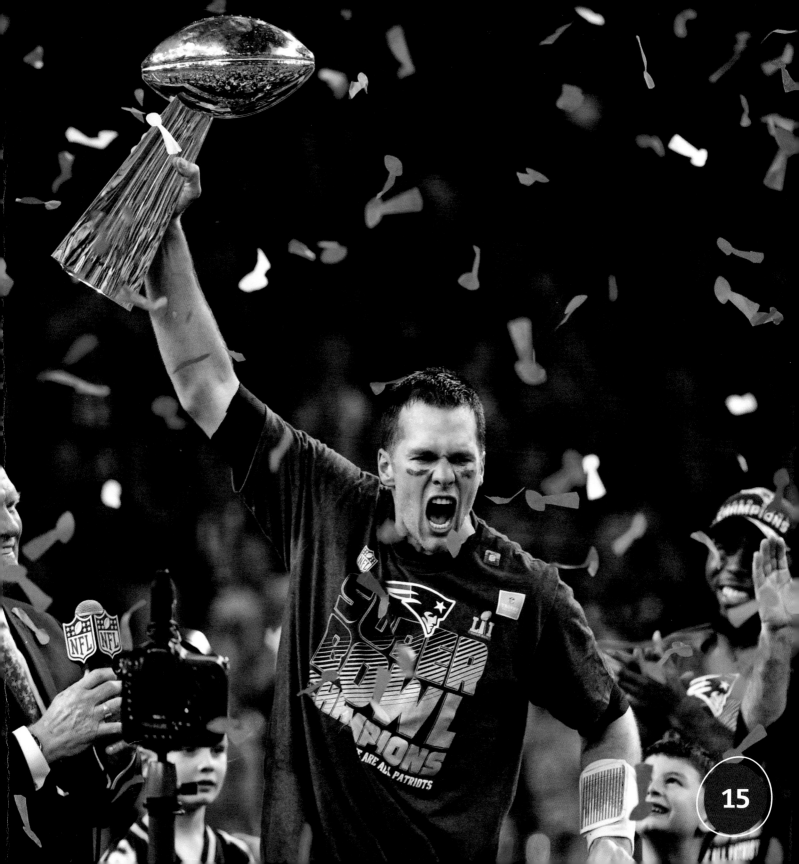

Some fans said Tom was the best

quarterback ever.

Tom gets lots of exercise.

He eats good food.

Tom stays strong and healthy.

He could win even more

Super Bowls!

Football Gear

football

jersey

pads

helmet

Picture Glossary

college

school after high school

exercise

work to make the body strong

fans

people who like a sport

quarterback

a football player who throws passes

Read More

Flynn, Brendan. *Football Time!* Minneapolis: Lerner Publications, 2017.

Kelley, K. C. *Tom Brady.* New York: Bearport, 2018.

Schuh, Mari. *Football.* Mankato, MN: Amicus, 2018.

Index

baseball, 7

college, 8

high school, 7

New England Patriots, 4, 11, 14

quarterback, 4, 11, 17

Super Bowl, 14, 20

Photo Credits

Image credits: Icons: Amy Salveson/Independent Picture Service; Focus on Sport/Getty Images, pp. 5, 6, 23 (bottom right); AP Photo/Scott Boehm, pp. 9, 23 (top left); Linda Cataffo/NY Daily News Archive/Getty Images, p. 10; John Tlumacki/The Boston Globe/Getty Images, pp. 13, 18–19, 23 (top right); TIMOTHY A. CLARY/AFP/ Getty Images, pp. 14–15; Jim Davis/The Boston Globe/Getty Images, pp. 16, 21, 23 (bottom left); Mtsaride/ Shutterstock.com, p. 22 (top left); Rob Marmion/Shutterstock.com, p. 22 (top right); dean bertoncelj/Shutterstock .com, p. 22 (bottom left); Beto Chagas/Shutterstock.com, p. 22 (bottom right).

Cover: Jim Rogash/Getty Images.